THE
HUNT
WITHIN

The Hunt Within

Poems by JAMES B. HALL

LOUISIANA STATE UNIVERSITY PRESS
Baton Rouge   1973

The poems published here have appeared previously in the following periodicals: *Accent, Perspective, Beloit Poetry Journal, Western Review, Poetry Northwest, Poetry* (Chicago), *West Coast Review, Sewanee Review, Malabat Review, Kayak,* and elswhere. "Four Necessary Encounters" appeared first in *Oregon Signatures,* a state centennial volume of Oregon poetry.

ISBN 0-8071-0059-5
Library of Congress Catalog Card Number 73-77651
Copyright © 1973 by James B. Hall
All rights reserved
Manufactured in the United States of America
Printed by Braun-Brumfield, Inc., Ann Arbor, Michigan
Designed by Dwight Agner

For my mother,
and to the memory of my father

CONTENTS

THE
HUNT
WITHIN

FOUR
NECESSARY
ENCOUNTERS

I Tortoise

Where hired men bent their backs
Along barbed wire
Across my father's partial soil
A tortoise it was
Old Lee pried from our fence row,
That blue-vine meridian,
When Elm trees blew the fifes of noon.

Tortoise of noon in the sun's shell,
Dated by carving,
Handed me there in the barbed
Wire fences of the sun
That March-day of tenants moving
When our line fences heaved
Beneath the flanks of another Spring.

Tortoise in hand before I knew
Only a tortoise shell
Held farm and fence and the high sullen
Dollar of the sun upon its back,
Dated by carving, yet dimly read
In the sun-fenced rows
To a boy's winking, reptile heart.

II Snake

Where the briar's rough caress
Begat indignant berries
For our casual harvest,
Where a white-oak stump
Burned in its old slow fire
Of moss, I saw her;

In the center of our woods
Where the lecher briars
Coupled with sumac,
Draping her folds of purple
Scaled-copper against the sky,
Molten and gorged, she slept.

Neither root nor hardpan shuddered
When her slow head
Swayed lewd among leaves
And her sly round reptile eye
Opened, but could not wink
Into the face of my trespass;

Old arts forgotten, she bestirred
Her slattern's flesh
And roiled across the sumac's roof
Seeking some deeper core of briar
To tell her slack-hide glozing mate
Of guile, seen lately in a boy's eye.

III Birds

Lapwing, the deceiver
Or the sneaking jay
A martin, purple
As muscadine
On our twittering vines,
Or a horse-turd sparrow
Wallowing the eye of God;

Peewee, the rain prophet,
Or the foraging crow,
The quail, harried by the sun,
Or the swallows at nest
Beshitting our barns;

Shikepoke, crane,
Or pigeons suspended
In that Ohio, pagan air:
Each beak pecked its bloody share
For each worm squealed
Beneath its sod or locust bark
Courting the fury of all meadow larks.

IV Boy (with himself)

Barbed wire rusts
In a tortoise sun
Beak by briar
May be undone;
What a boy needs know
Need be learned again:
That Winter makes snow,
And Spring makes rain.

THE
KNIGHT

Steel encased, the knight rides
Out into the busy world.
It's all out there:
The day and the valley,
Foe, friend, the meal in the hall;
And the maid, the wood, the month of May—
Yes, and the Holy Grail
And in all the streets
In a thousand ways, God shows himself.

Yet, also inside the armor of the knight,
Inside those sinister rings,
Death squats, musing and brooding:
When will the sword, that strange
Liberating blade, spring
Over the iron hedge
To release *me* from this place
That has cramped me many a day
So that I can stretch myself
   And play
        And sing.

(translated from the German
of Rilke: *Das Buch der Bilder*)

HOW
TO MAKE
THE POEM

Now a good job
Wants the prime, vicious timbers
With no gum, or snarl-eyed grain
Giving purchase when an ungreased axle
Grinds smoke from the hub's core,
    In these times of winter;
So with the spokeshave and the auger's
Crafty tongue, I contrive or warp
This oak: by fire blown on steel,
    And the hulked anvil heel

Center hub and spoke
Inside a rim's hot comprehension,
And look now, Brother, at this wheel:
She tracks in thresher's dust and through the mire
Of pigs, or weathers only in a barnyard
    Reviled by sparrows.
No matter, that stuff stood in these woods
Suckled by roots sunk through the old debris
Of glaciers, grew by connivance with this sun,
    And so I think she'll hold.

But moment is place only,
This birth by spoke or word is like
A flint's revenge upon some sullen log
Scraped in fire to make canoes of war:
Mound Builder, Shawnee, what of your cries
    Which named the sun
Towards morning? Therefore take me, tusk's
Destruction, adze edge, or even the martin's
Hacking wing: crush me wheel, your maker,
    Into this drift of meadow.

IN
BAILEY
WOODS

Oh young my farmer
Blood and nine, so I leaped
To hear our dogs break the barnyard
Kennels, the limping fox crouched in their eyes,
And Redbone's nostril eager for the split entrails,
In Bailey's woods;

Then mother, goodbye:
For somewhere in our swamps
A bitch-fox shudders in her hollow log
While dogs lope through the scrub oak grove,
Answering the horn's throat and following call,
Through Bailey woods.

My nine summers
Stretched their shadow on that cleared
November earth, hearing the bitch-fox
And dogs trailing, until the reeling swamp beneath
My ear's rapt corridor was like a wheel humming
In Bailey woods;

And there in trees
Old Redbone bayed away
His hunting heart, and fell. The fox
Circled, circled that ranging night away and trailed
The pack, back-tracked into a reach of Sandy Creek
And there through briars

Watched the dogs
Bury flank and steaming tits
Deep in the slough and sand bars of that
Creek, until they shook the dawn in water spangles
From their wet backs, and lost the trail
In Bailey woods.

Therefore much I
Hunted on patrol, beyond barbed
Wire into a dark Alsatian night
Where the flare, slipped by the Very Pistol's throat
Bayed night away, and the Corporal screamed his winter,
In some other woods;

But I am nine
And forty, now, and want to hear
The hounds' crossed bones bay through the swamp
To rustle my brain's black burnt-out timber lands
For once the hunter, bitch, pack, and swamps were one,
In Bailey woods.

THE
FIRE
WINDER

Fire melts wood, and frost shall freeze
This blossom, earth. And the ice
Shall bridge water and seize
The earth's growth, budding. But one
Shall unbind the snow's embrace: Christ
The fair weather, the summer-hot sun
Returns, and the cunning restless sea.

(from *The Exeter Gnomes*, adaptation from Old English)

THE
FRISIAN
WIFE

Welcome her lover to the Frisian wife
When ship is at anchor, the sailor home;
Her own food-giver, contriving this life.
Wash the wave-stained garments alone,
Give him upon waking the clean raiment. The shore
Is sweet when thoughts are by love
Restrained, and woman should wait the more
For her man, nor shame him; and above
All be not reeling, but steadfast, nor
Woo the horseback man, when her lord is away.
Often the sea keeps the sailor long, therefore
He sights only the sea's old dismay,
Containing the wind, that shall not speed.
But the day comes when he steers to the land
Alive and warm and taut with his old need—
Or deep sea holds him, with clutching hand.

(from *The Exeter Gnomes*, adaptation from Old English)

11

SEASONAL

Consider the cardinal's withdrawn
Swaying nest contrived from burning
Straws and the wing fluttering a spawn
Of sunlight, while the sapling

Shakes in the harsh frog note
Of Spring; yet bringing, in season,
This boy whistling Fall's old hope
Of harvest, devouring that sun

Caught now in fallen paw-paws.
His foot, sliding in
Silence, climbs upward to behold
Nested wreckage: old shells smitten

From within by the yellow beaks,
Or rains of early Winter.
Unseen the nearby falling leaves
Speak protection to the coiling pups

Whimpering in the red-fox den,
Gnawing again their chicken bones. Nor sound
Of his own dog shall waken him
This night, digging the yellow ground.

THE
HUNT
WITHIN

That hill
Is humped raising its weight
Of snows towards the sun
That burns away the high fog, the dawn
Of a new mid-winter

And the scrub pine
Bristles on that hill's back
Like hackles while the hound
Digs memory's root of a fox dead
Or bone forgotten.

Now the picket
Crow calls black and clarion
Through these encircling woods
And the last dry berry of summer trembles
And drops in moss

While my dog
Grovels the hillock's bluest snow
Whimpering from his forepaw's
Slit tenderness. Now this gun's
Full-primed,

Eager shells
Ram home to their steel chamber,
And I want to see
A man crouched or through briars running,
To shoot him dead,

Like any game.
Therefore I hunt through sumacs
On the dirty little footprints
Of revenge and maim even the snipe's
Slack-wing flutter,

Explode the squirrel's
Grey brief chattering hide,
For vengeance on this land
Burns, Oh bloody and firm beneath
This hunting jacket,

Revenge upon
This souring land that made me.
    Now the hound claws
The entrails of the hill, the whipping briar
        Fires my eye

        And the tear
From the thorn or the wind only
    Makes course through these hackles
On my cheek, snuffling to answer the ancient
        Baying dog within.

GASPAR'S FERRY:
END OF
OHIO ROADS

Slashed first by trapper, wide as my father's boot
The valley roads now are pounded white,
Widened by dragged log, survey and wheels to bright
Concrete, now ends yet marked as shortest routes:

To a County Home that hides my Uncle's eye
Which sees in every car some fleeing chicken thief,
But gums his memory only after meals and cries
Or beats with cane on pipes to call again for heat;

To cemeteries deep grown as fields where
Tractors heave up the sod of Indian mounds,
Forgotten, except by the sassafras root and briars,
For bones do not hurdle barrow stones.

Or, also lost at night, some old man drives
Our roads from curve to crossroads then must stop
At a house to ask the way, but cannot make
The porch for dogs patrol the gate, locked.

Endless now are all the towns and roads from them
Each road more narrow, until hikers who seek a
Short cut from Jimtown Pike to a lane by Little Scarum
Find the cow path becomes a raccoon track in sand of creek;

Therefore we drive and towards the end of season
By Gaspar's Ferry cross to Old Kentucky,
Darkandbloody, where the hills muse and darkly
Gape at matches we light to find the entrance to a park,
And there beyond paths we wander and in a gully
Stumble on the facedown corpse of all our picnic visions.

GRANDMOTHER

Calls now for husband
But he no more drops
The hames or a bent coupling pin
To answer the voice of her cane
Thumping across the porch floor
to fetch him;

Calls now for her dinner
But cannot remember
How just now her porridge steamed
While the old growl inside her
Sucked spoon, then gnawed the bowl,
Or so it seemed.

She rocks upon the sills
Of all past anger, powerless
While the weed patch of her brain
Blossoms again with memories of a small
Livery stable near the depot
And how in the rain

He drove the small bay
Gelding out at midnight to cart
Those trollop nuns to St. Martin's,
And how near daylight she lashed him into straw
With a buggy whip, let blood later,
With her jealous tongue.

Stares now beyond
Those old Sunday lawns of memory
Into the autumn field which lay
More wrinkled and shrunk than bee-stung plums
There sees her own decaying face
In the senile clay.

Yet turns to business,
And while hills doze in this sun
Like simpletons she thumps for tea,
And with the cunning of the very old
Shows all her sly, antique buttons
She has bequeathed to me.

PILGRIMS:
UNCLE SID

In water there is recognition
And therefore my Uncle Sid
Stared something less than forty years
Into a falling, or a rising, reservoir.

When the B & O dammed up a reach
Of Honey Creek they took him on,
When young, to lower or to raise
Their floodgates, according to season,

And so my Uncle Sid arose
And walked out each winter day
Six miles to work, and then walked back
A watcher of water, and sometimes small carp.

But good only as a watcher
Of water, it was well said,
For in the droughts of summer
He slept upright, on an old nail keg,

And being twice bought, he elected
Not to fish, or vote, or even speak
Until at last it was well said
That he, himself, was much like water.

After something less than forty years
He died one night, in his house,
In his own bed, grim to the very end
When his own sluice gates sprung

Inside the reaches of his own lungs
And uncaged that vast calamity of waters
Which cleansed not much at all from his wallet
Then flooded forever the mud flats of his brain.

THE
TENANT

At the wood's edge
The terrain once more familiar
I squatted by a leaf-shaped pool
—Not daring to drink,
The ground fog dissembling among roots—
There stared at my own face
Held in the fork of my own legs
Face, and legs forked, my billed cap
Shivering with the ferns in that refracted wind.

Held in the dull
Escrow of all stagnant water
I saw the small fungus on my lips
—From sleeping in leaves,
The hedgehogs digging past midnight—
Yet there I remained until frost
Flowed west along the barbed wire
Towards the road: each dawn I embraced
The delirium of moss, but ate little.

Before the first snows,
My shotgun rusted at half-cock,
I left those encircling woods
—Had lived on elderberries
The sun forever threshing the sky—
Yet remembering well the summer past
When in the sheet lightning of dreams
I floated like a vast grey squirrel
Across the smoke and oak stumps of those nights.

At home once more
Among the dark catalepsy of your barns
I manage the new foreclosures of winter
—Yet note the six Durocs well fed out,
The wife already boiling my shave water—
A winter at hand when even the rioting
Blue shadows of all your mice shall freeze.
But landlords, listen, your woods are also burning.
I say it honestly, who each spring travel there.

MY
FATHER

In Florida the occult cry of birds
Swings like a net above the trailer parks
Where men talk weather, and stare,
And horseshoes, spinning, score the hours.
Yet, even in Florida, the antique snows
Of memory still fall across his heart.

Once more my Father smells the thunder
Of sunshine beyond his old Ohio furrows
Where his earth-tramper Percherons
Drove plowshares through a killdeer's nest,
Where, in later years, his Fordson
Tractors shook the roots of his own woods.

Oh, he was just among his own barns:
To all weevils, subtle in wheat, the gas;
To fence-rooter shoats, the ring;
To clay land, clover; to a swamp more lime;
To women, right tools, and to all men
Who worked, good food enough at noon.

Towards evening, four nights a week, to town:
Genial in pool room or at a church bazaar
He flexed credit like a flail for his good word
Was gold, and the rummy deck leaped lightly
In his hand until as Master-All-Worshipful,
He made Tau his lodge doors against the world.

But now he sits in Florida where orange
Trees grow skyward under a reeking sun
And the gaping, bright-gilled tourists
Feed on the palm tree's habit-forming shade—
Yet from the throat of every grim hibiscus hears
A cut-shoat's gelded scream.

Of course he knows this mindless sun
Is only show, and he knows the squirming
Everglades must sometime invade his green,
Mismanaged rooms. But in his customary way
Rolls once and with his face towards the wall
Accepts in sleep the vast black wink of night.

In that resinous dark, while his heart
Hammers the old catastrophe of blood through veins,
He can not dream. Instead he thinks upon
A crossroad, a wreck, and a daughter, dead,
And of his son who sometimes ships a box of pears
From Oregon or towards midnight may telephone, collect.

CONFERENCE TIME;
OR, THE
UNDERGROUND AGENTS

Between classes
Outside this basement room the vines.
Mew in the sunlight and tendrils
Pry at the ignorant glass while student
Feet, all mismated, snuffle
The sidewalk towards Biology;
    Across the hall,

The casts rattle
In the bonepile cast museum
And Zeus braces his buttocks
Against a civil servant's feather duster
While I, a poet in waiting,
Affect the double jeopardy of sleep
    Perhaps to lure

A phrase which will rave
Or will swing like the black
Bat's wing, or will grow within
Round as a wen, and so become
The rubber detonator, soft in the pocket,
Armed, quivering, ready to explode
    The infernal mirrors

Of all the keepers
Of our poetry in poetry's Managerial Age.
Now the class bells ring and Keats
Writhes again beneath a New Instructor's
Well-trained sneer, or a pedant leers
Above the works of John Clare's
    Giddy hours

Smiling the kill,
"Gentlemen: could he *really*, if mad?"
Soon the Tartar fullbacks' overriding
Thunder shall benumb these corridors
As they come, repentant and sly, to examinations.
Good sleep takes the knitting girls,
    And no one reads.

Comes now the hour
Of conspirators for outside the door
My student-poet stands, conjuring
Still the forbidden delicacy of flight
With last night's poems concealed
Beneath his sullen leather jacket,
        These muddy cyphers

        Pried last night
From underneath the terrible boards
Of memory: the Viet Nam night attack
Against a jungle's automatic weapons
Or the week his brother died so slowly
Of pneumonia in a cold farm house.
        His poems are here

        Squarely between us,
The revised emblems of our redemption,
And on Page Three I read, "The lilies
Rustled then bloomed like fires of Hell,
Or tracer bullets." There I see
The squirm of talent which will surely bore
        Like a spirochete

        Devouring at last
Even the great tendons of his pride.
Zeus rattles and all the tendrils dive
But this new poet smells my death
And imperiously rattles his verses.
We leave as friends, but I go to connive
        In committee meeting.

WINE OF
ALGERIA:
1942

One German held the vats of that cold-walled
Winery but he left before our half-track
With antennae and three guns waving crawled
Among the orange trees by the wall in back

And parked concealed. Inside we bought the wine can
Which held five gallons for the three of us.
We understood enough to know that Germans
Drank little but saluted much, took pulp

Seeds, wine, and by distillation made
Fuel from the grapes and by this chemistry
Mounted Stukas from the desert into the sun to raid
The parapets of our indug artillery

Camouflaged with nets, in low hills concealed,
Except to one pilot who on orders steered
Strafing into our flak. We saw him reel
And like an armored screaming stallion rear,

Pawing at the sun, then spin and splash
Those vineyards with blood and fuel, the plan
And order of their rage. But that crash
Was past, so we drank and sang and drank again

While a woman peered down from her barred
Window at our sagged bodies and our fire.
By noon someone awoke, and we cut our
Trembling fingers on ration tins. Then with warmed-up

Motor we left to search again through fields
For our lost Headquarters and while we cursed
We saw the vineyard and the orange groves reel
Stopped then, and puked our policy back upon their earth.

ON
PAY DAY
NIGHT

Picture a desert and the *Panzer* man
Goggled even in death by his ruthless
Sun glasses, obeying a last command

To hold a mortar pit though his roofless
Head sucked sand as our platoon
(Aware then only a little of the careless

Sirocco) wondered why—so soon—
Our replacements joined us. But this
Is scarcely remembered for the loom

Of memory creaks and our old tricks,
Such as those grenades of phosphorus
Tossed scalding into bunkers near Bitche,

Fade nicely; by now it was not us
At all for, like juries, can a platoon
Remember? Happy we are that the rust

Hulk sinks, that Victory is a room
Of some weather station where the godless
Anemometer whines, spinning its doom

By consort with storms. Now, careless
Of policy, we froth this bar with our
Spigot laughter and in darkness caress

The purple flesh of conscience for we are
Old He Ones, so heads I win
A pack of Chesters—and we know The Saar

Is no damned good. Now our gin
And tonics roar at closing time, now
Shall any man forget that day in

Basic that we donned Europe's head, bowed
Into our gas masks and took that gas
Which trained us; saw in a mirror how

Our heads were not bird or fish, or brass
Of Idols, that wagging tube no tongue
To speak, nor beak to shatter glass

For here the goggle, head, and mask were one,
Faceless, no sting, no tear, no sound nor laughter:
We clawed, came out like reptiles—not wise, not
    young.

MEMORIAL DAY: 1959

I

When the long iron boat spat us kicking
On the beach near Mers El Kebir
The sea birds twittered past our let-down
Ramp and we ran laughing at a continent,
Not one truly thinking he could die;
But now I think of Elwood Matson
Surprised that night in his own bivouac
Hole, tent poles and his own Garrand
Gouged through his blanket and his blond head,
For a tank track foraged through the lost
Field of his sleep.

II

And A. C. Roten: often he danced
On our tent ropes and would sometimes sing
Those low, cold Tunisian stars to sleep.
Married, a picture of small girls hiding
In his wallet, and lucky at reconnaissance,
I did not think that he could ever be
Only some rags at Senid Station, thighs severed,
His throat screaming for its mother . . .
And later Graysted, Kibby, Ethred, and Sidney Hines
Died also by S-mines in the Riviera's green
Unforgiving afternoon.

III

Much later winter came on us near Hagenau
And the season's old revenge of snow shook
The black intricate trees like thunder.
Beaton, and his patrol, in parkas white as breath
Vanished into those mumbling, low-hung boughs.
Later we found them in a shallow bowl
Of that forest, swaying, trussed in the wind,
Flanks maimed, their heads drowned in the terrible snow.
After that we took no prisoners, fought much
Among ourselves with knives, became beasts,
But still, alive.

IV

Now is this longest day of May again
And while the shrapnel rain rattles this window pane,
I thought to write some formal thing
To say how those alive—being so—see on ahead,
And thought that way to justify their sleep.
But oh when I saw them all once more, again,
I thought: write no lies to those who really died.
Instead let stand this hasty parapet of verse:
For A. C. Roten, Ethred, Matson, Kibby, Graysted,
Paul Sommers, Sindey Hines, John Halstead, and one patrol,
For they are dead.

METROPOLITAN

Our place is sales
A space enclosed by walls
An office bordered by promotions:
But once in rain our cheeks touched and bruised
When my car skidded and one balding
Tire proved guard rails only guard
The curve's defection.

No matter now
For Love came to Accounting
Unpackaged there, and even the office
Boy squeezing his pimples at the washroom mirror
Knew: yet though tethered and reviled
Our bruise closed with fruition in this
Malicious centering.

In sickness or
In health therefore I
Take thee to where our scarecrow
Lamps shall frighten peepers—but our In-Laws'
Shower-gifts surround and bind us
While a mouse tail quivers towards his trap
For food, libation.

AFTER HIS
POETRY
READING

Shortly past midnight Stafford left the party
Their questions not answered, but his poetry read.
Alone, he walked down the rained-on steps
And Kester Svendsen's house lights shook,
Then burned like brandy flames behind the shrubbery.

At the curb, rat-grey in the moonlight,
The car waits patiently as an old dray horse,
Moves at last, then goes stomping away
Towards the Portland Freeway where trucks
Bore holes through ground fogs as they go.

To the north the towns are crusts of light,
And off there no doubt some stranded tourist
Might identify himself and with his wife
Claim shelter in Tangent or beyond Sweet Home
The hour and a credit card notwithstanding.

Ahead, above a hillock's moonlit woods,
Stafford sees this floating, windshield vision:
A great white barn, opulent beneath clouds,
Hip-roofed, corporate, fat as any ram,
But he believes this thing is only a version

Of Kansas where the men's work all that summer
Brought only the sky's own slave-whip lightning,
Flayed joists, sills, roof, and their mowed hay
Until flames scorched even the women with water buckets—
Yes, eight brood sows lost, and two fine horses.

But Kansas, that burned-out recollection of barns,
is not Oswego: home now, this side of sunrise,
Stafford parks at the curb of their paid-off house,
And thinks Dorthy no doubt is still awake
And is—in fact—one end to every reading;

There beneath the porch light, but beyond
The reprieve of ashes, Stafford looks into the sky,
Sees the black stallion belly of our northwest
Weather running, sees a starlit, terrible dynasty
Well harnessed, and good enough to work tomorrow.

MAN
BETWEEN
CORNERS

The sea cannot converse with any scarlet fish
Nor keel of skiff with spiders on this sand
For words of other worlds lack the valence of release,
Therefore caulk the boundaries, contain the single man;

Still, your glance makes a quadrant of each dream
Which makes survey of all tides beneath my skin
Shows spindrift nerves break running on my brain
Where it is known the landslips of an end begins.

DEATH,
BY
HOT ROD

At midnight what skid or puncture of desire
Dared you race the cams of Time and flame
Your engines out of laughter until the fire
Of speed consumed the brain, and pain
Released the head, now upholstered in the rain?

Midnight, and you drive a road that writhes
And sow a wheel on which the swerve depends,
Rend metal bright as horses scream through sky
And wake the farmer who by telephone can only send
For State Patrol or relay cries to fathers who attend
The flow of oxygen, or puzzle over lights
That were switched off, and hear the Doctor's sigh.

Now, as overcoated men compelled to view our crime
(Or for report) stand marble-footed in this frost
To reconsider, after shock, these ruins chocked in Time:
Of youth whose orbits lay in wheels, who thought
Asteroids could not collide in worlds so lost,
Who can not hear some old garageman from his wrecker say,
"Stand back, men, we got to haul these stripped-down
     wrecks away."

DRESSING
YOUR
DEER

The season opened at dawn
    and you just killed your first deer.

First, cut its throat crosswise
    to sever the jugular vein;
If, however, your deer's blood is not circulating
    this will not be necessary.

Now:
    through the skin,
    but not into the body cavity,
    between hams and base of the throat,
    make your next incision
        (at this point the brisket
        is very handily opened
        by either a saw or an axe)
    for this allows the windpipe,
        esophagus,
            lungs,
                and
                      heart
    to be removed very readily.

Next:
    while you cut through
    muscle and tissues
    into the body cavity
    observe the diaphragm—
    the thing which separates
        heart and lungs
    from the stomach of your deer.
    Cut this diaphragm muscle
        very carefully
        and *completely* around
    your deer's body cavity.
    Only now are you ready
    to remove the entire viscera.

All ready?
    Begin
        with the windpipe
    and then
        the esophagus,
            lungs
                liver
                    heart
                        stomach
                            intestines.
    (Keep the liver and heart
    clean: of this, more later.)

In addition:
    we have the problem
    of the bladder and colon:

    now I've always thought
    this was best accomplished
    by either a saw or an axe,
    but be careful: break the bladder
    and you spoil the hams
    for they will taste strong.

A minor point:
    remove any tissues
    spoiled by your shot.

Now skin your deer:
    hang by the head
    then make incisions
        down
            the inside
            of the front
            and of the hind
                legs.

In conclusion:
     your deer can now be quartered
     and hung each night in the fresh air
     or placed in fly-proof bags in the daytime;
     you can get home even in hot weather
     with sweet, fine meat each hunting season
     if your animal
     is dressed out properly
     and the animal heat cooled at once from the carcass.
     On the contrary,
     any deer left with its entire viscera
     even in high pine woods can sour;
     follow these easy directions
     and your meat
     will never taste wild or strong.
One final thing:
     about that liver and heart
     you were careful to keep *clean*.

     Always take these things home,
     cut the liver into medium-sized strips,
     and inspect for larvae, flukes, and so on.

     Towards evening, in your back yard,
     light up your charcoal grille
     and add a few green twigs
     to send up much smoke.

     Then call in all
     your neighborhood boys
     and see how they like to eat
     the clean heart and the clean liver
     especially when served almost raw.
As for explanations—
     should anyone bother to ask—
     tell them this:

     God put all creatures
     on this earth
     for your right use.

MOBY
JANE

I

Legend and rumors at sea
Told Moby Dick of Ahab's
Bright unconditional lance
And of the *Pequod*'s holy fires;

His goal was always Truth
And so, to gather evidence,
He swam from our beds of kelp
And the new calf at my dugs.

Each night for one month
He spied upon the *Pequod*'s decks
Yet saw only unnatural acts,
Obsession, an old man going mad;

Rightly he judged those things
Trivial, or merely secondary
To the *Realpolitik* of headlands,
Or the comprehensive depths of the sea.

II

On the third day, only to resolve
That morbid chase, he turned back
And stove the *Pequod*, yet left
One man afloat to tell their story;

For years, at home, the old harpoons
Rusted his innocent, white flanks,
But some say Ahab's steel also touched
His mind: now full of ambergris
He calculated order in flotsam,
In dreams, saw all-white continents—
And yet, there was no real malice in him.

The glass fell in the solstice of his years:
In winter he forged to the north, half-blind
By the storm's dark sea-heave spumes—
And grounded off Kodiak. From that reef

All night he preached One World and Love
To sea lions at rut and also unaware
Of men with clubs, at hunt for pelts,
Waiting for dawn to break on that barking shore.

DRAGON

I

Our fight was more than fair
The day I—Volant—descried
The knight's lance-tip in sunlight

Advancing towards me on the plain;
Being at hunt, for food,
I had no real obligation

To dip my wing's hot shadow
And arouse the horse
And Knight to honest combat.

I say, "more than fair"
For each claimed advantage
Of his natural element:

The knight elected earth,
And armor; but I, Volant, I
Was somewhat quicker in the air.

His first charge failed,
And then my kill was clean;
Being at hunt, I stripped

The meat from horse and man
And with the armor on my back
Flew—not hungry—to my lair.

II

Life, itself, of course went on
And in my turn I judged
Our youth in trials of Abstinence

High in the Hartz Mountains
Among our customary barrows;
There I saw my own son

Take vows to guard forever
Our great glittering gold hoards
From night attack by serpents.

Meanwhile, in the way of old mementos
His lance and armor rusted in my cave—
In short, I thought no more about it.

III

Now, honored among barrows,
Their burned haystacks all behind me,
Their scopes at song in every Abbey

Chimney corner tell their nuns I lost:
Yes, say I, Volant, lost that day
To "virtue" and to the knight's renunciation.

True, the thing took place long ago
Yet I still believe our fight was fair:
I broke lance and horse, and took the meat.

Beyond those facts, I see no conclusion
Except I say that day real Virtue
Died, and the Seven Easy Sins took over.

SPOOR

I Dog

I say there's cruelty
Beneath tolerance and I say affection
Is the shoe that kicks your ribs

But to tell the truth I run
Beneath my clothes line of necessity
And thus avoid their grocery trips:

They park me with the car
Then bring back meat in paper sacks
Easy to rip—but always out of reach.

And I say there's cruelty
In those cans of "doggie" food
They fetch to me: suet and liver

Warmed but not quivering
Like good live meat tracked
Then killed by my own illicit teeth.

Oh, towards nightfall I patrol
Their shrubs and can pretend
To guard their eunuch flower beds,

And I've known some foolish dogs
Who yelped in fields beneath the moon,
But I would not advise it.

Coyotes skulk in those hedge rows
And kill all dogs very slowly—
When it's safe. And as for rutting

Why I know six bitch dogs
Within one hot mile of here
All easy to mount, and all spayed.

Still you have to live some way
So I have learned to lick a hand:
It's expected, and helps avoid the pound.

I say if dogs had hands for paws
We'd soon see who barked in pens
Near laboratories—evolution notwithstanding.

39

As for facts, I know my Vet is fast
(He's only in it for the money)
So a dog's life is that, and nothing more.

Meanwhile my creed is this: Defile
Their roses every chance and live
To kill the Persian cat which sleeps next door:
A dog's life is only that, and nothing more.

II Cat

Why should I stir from my warm place
For all the world outside? I like silk,
And our rug with tufts of white is Grace

Enough for me. What's more, my milk's
Homogenized and my basket's always clean;
It's true I simply will not sleep on quilts

And it's been years since any raucous, obscene
Flea shuttled through my well-combed fur.
You see, I'm certain things are what they seem

And so I smile and watch that little cur
Across the street—yes, smile—for *it* barks,
Defiles their roses, growls at food, is vulgar

Beyond belief. I say my own remarks
Confirm good breeding and of course
I do have papers. I say my thought marks

Well a sensual, Persian mind which the hoarse
Paws of Airedales shall not put down. It's right
That I should live forever, *sans* remorse:

> *Give us our fish in our clean dish*
> *Make ladies whisper, when we're asleep*
> *Give us our basket, give us dry heat*
> *Forgive us the dust which corrupts our feet.*

Oh, as for children
    I've heard
        They're a lady's delight,

But not—please—
    By a Tom
        Under shrubbery at night.

III Coyote

    The night
Stalks from these foothills
Mouth-dark and more silent
    Than any cougar

    But I
Am scabbed by ticks, my guts
Burn in the night-thirst of rabies
    And so, alone,

    I die
Beyond my pack's old authority.
Yet once they harried the landscape
    At my back

    And I
Led them down the neon throat
Of suburbs and saw my shadow leap
    Like a scythe blade

    Over fences.
There we ate filth from garbage cans
And broke the backs of Airdales
    Where they whined.

    Now I
See rabid visions of the night,
See certain, new, unleashed authority
    To be seized by cunning.

    Oh on
That day I shall command these hills
To convulse, to send out packs not yet dreamed
    By grocery shoppers;

I shall
Lope howling down the overwhelming
Sky and shall upheave the pipes of sewers
From their graves.

That day
I shall be sleek as a tank car
Followed by the bitch pack running,
Each one in heat;

That day
No child or wheel-chair cripple
Shall escape this Joy you now see in me.
Until then, wait.

NINE BRIGHT IDEAS
FOR SPRING
With Apologies to *Family Life.*

1. Plant a Small Herb Garden

Start thyme, basil, and sage
Each in a sunny pot
And reserve some space
For a Junior Herb Garden:
All little girls will love you for it.

2. Visit Your State Capitol

First, write for an appointment
With your Senior Senator;
And remember to order passes
For the House Visitor's Gallery:
All little boys will love you for it.

3. Go on a Dandelion Hunt

Treat kids to an old-time outing,
Make their greens into a springy salad;
Wash all leaves in luke-warm water,
Toss until everything wilts slightly.
All small worms will love you for it.

4. Build a Simple Birdbath

Surround some water with rocks
(as shown in the above illustration)
But avoid shrubbery or trees
That might hide naughty cats:
Certain sparrows will love you for it.

5. Erect Windowsill Flagpoles

First obtain two smallish flags
From almost any automobile supply store—
Or two kits may be even better:
Bracket, gromets, rope, pulley-wheel. Install.
Patriots in Florida will love you for it.

6. Get Acquainted with the Stars

Spring nights give us constellations
But best use a simple star chart and pointer;
First locate the real Big Dipper,
Then read them the myth of Orion the Hunter.
Astronomers, nationwide, will love you for it.

7. Adopt an Artist

Rembrandt, Wyeth, Mary Cassatt,
Read everything you can about them;
Then buy a few reproductions and don't be
Surprised if all Art *seems much closer*.
If alive, Van Gogh would love you for it.

8. Attend Religious Services of Another Faith

The ecumenical view begins at home,
So build better understanding
        Among all church goers;
Little girls should prepare to cover
Their heads if their thoughts are Episcopalian
        Or even Roman Catholic.
The preachers in Heaven will love you for it.

9. Finally, Make May Baskets

Some rainy afternoon revive
This ancient custom: tell everyone
To place them on the doors of neighbors;
Yes, even on the slammed doors of those
Who say he never will come back
To this large, almost paid-for house.
Someday, almost for sure, almost forever
Little girls and little boys will love you for it.

SONG:
SUNDAY UP
THE RIVER

When the crocus sights the Spring
Its yellow cup to warmth raising
And the martin's purple wing
Slips the wind by feathers singing
Then we shall lie on this green grass all day
Stroking, Oh lightly, our stringed holiday.

Yet this Spring consorts with snow
Its vagrant warmth came from below
And the tiger lily snaps its bee,
Gone stamen and bloom, the pod's misery.
And we shall be under this used grass all day
Crying, Oh darkly, that winter away.

So drink our up-tipped yellow glass
Lips parted drink purple, drink off this day:
Spread suddenly your long green hair on this grass
Speak sunshine, Oh brightly, by your tongue's disarray.

A CLUTCH
OF DREAMS

The forked path in the woods
Dreams of a crossroads,
A perfection in concrete, dividing
This valley into four equal fields;

The shoat at the slaughterhouse door
Remembers a fine white gate
At the barn-end of a meadow
And corn calling with the voice of a man.

Waterlogged, the orange liferaft
Drifts on the wide-eyed Pacific
Then sinks, still dreaming of atolls,
And the new crew roistering ashore.

And I, on this forked path
Of dreams, I see fine white gates
And I ride this orange-raft world
Downward towards coral, where all dreams end.

IN THE COMPOUNDS
OF ERROR
(after Saneatsu)

Judas

They are saying I hanged myself?
Well, sit down—have a sherbert. Here,
You take my seat. Of course I'm happy
To tell you everything I ever knew
About Jesus, and I'll give you names
Of gentlemen who will absolutely verify
What I say. They really will.

My little place? This little garden?
Oh, I like privacy, and speaking
Very, very frankly the lady here
Needs me—ah—to do her rents.
And I need a little leisure
To sit in her garden and someday
Gather opinions, to set the record straight.

I see what you're thinking:
My lit-tle fee. Oh, I sensed it.
Of course I took my fee—
No! Never did attempt to hang myself!
Much, *much* less than that . . .
People will exaggerate, you know.
Besides my fee is not the issue. Right?

For background, say I've slept late
These past six months. Her garden
Really is a satisfaction: we eat
Melon at ten, and on sunny days
I walk beside these walls
In meditation. Gardens do that to me
For, like yourself, I really am an intellectual.

Another cup of wine . . . No?
Well, then first put down this:
I still love him—I really do—
In most respects. His faults,
And here I'm being very candid,
Were of intellect. When you listened
Everything was fine. But what then?

Of all the men around him
(More people left towards the end
Than is generally known) I alone
Dealt in issues that were real.
Actually, he needed someone like me,
Otherwise he became too ethereal,
And made all things seem less than real.

You see precisely what I mean?
Good, then consider just one thing:
Veracity. At first I was attracted
By the idea of God's kingdom. But
Was it here, or not? If after death
—A cunning doctrine—then where?
Naturally he always glossed that point over.

Or, let's make a clear distinction:
We have rhetoric and cunning;
But there are minds—like ours.
He, himself, said it, "Be cunning
As serpents," for cunning (not brains)
Was his strength. This could offend
For I wanted forthright answers. You see?

Assuredly, Sir, there is a lit-tle
Vanity in everyone. But he was also
Obstinate and could not recognize
Wisdom in other people. Example:
The Pharisees. They could have helped
But he said the same old thing:
"Oh ye of little faith." His mace,

His crutch. For what it's worth
That phrase would make your epigraph,
For we all know it was his answer
To any disagreement, as though he
Were a law against dissent.
"Oh ye of little faith" was useful
But just hear, from me, the consequence.

Thereby he asked only obeisance,
With no thought process implied:
Fishermen, etc., had merely to assent.
Dogmatic he was, but not himself genteel;
Really thoughtful minds could despise
him. So his followers were ignorant,
Or criminals, with no feelings of their own.

"Oh ye of little faith." Why I well
Remember it like bells, or palm fronds swinging.
By that imperative he monopolized
God for himself. Example:
In the wilderness. And then he said
Salvation came only if he, himself,
Were—in his own illogical way—respected.

Now quote me on this accurately:
"When he took God for himself,
Judas gradually decided to withdraw."
Yes "gradually" . . . to avoid embarrassments,
That fee was really only a symbol.
Moreover Jesus said he, alone,
Was God. That way he kept his flatterers.

Would you read that back?
Now let's state something else:
"Practical considerations came next.
Namely, the work could not succeed."
His people were dirty and I for one
Was embarrassed to work with them,
Though the poor sometimes were too good.

Often at night besides a wall
Or in some corner near a garden
Our meetings brought out a feeling
In me that anyone would remember
With affection. And I do remember.
I have no hatred, really.
They merely had no power. Were not wise.

So much for items of policy.
Of course he did not *manage* well.
Oh yes, it was all so emotional! . . .
Exactly what I wanted to touch on:
Women. We must really consider women.
In them you find the index
Of a man. Now regards Jesus and women.

Women, he liked. Perhaps too much.
With men, of course, he was severe,
And said if a disciple ever looked,
It was adultery. Whether in this way
Jesus also committed adultery
I would not know. But he liked women.
If they left his side, he was displeased.

Or this one: remember the woman
Who washed his feet, and dried them
With her hair? Just confidentially,
I saw it myself. Was there. He liked
That hot little extravagance. Said her
Act would "live." I think we can say
Jesus, the man, was too self-centered.

In short, I do not yet believe
He was a Savior. His teachings were . . .
Too commonplace, had no economic basis.
In fifty or sixty years I daresay
His "thought" will be out of fashion.
For the great things of our age
We must read and re-read the Pharisees.

Sympathize? I most certainly do.
At times I think that cross was pretty brutal,
But inevitable really, when he named
Himself sole Master. No, no regrets.
I was stupid then, but no more.
One's own education can be
Relevant to History. And after all who knows?

Plans? Well, you can state this:
First, I'll lay aside some money.
And then I'll form an organization
And prove that two can play his game,
But I'll reform the world. I mean
The real reforms of land and tax and rent.
So judge not, until you hear some more. From me.

John

All night I write
Letters and towards dawn
Our messengers depart.
I take a horn of water
But these days eat very little

And seldom sleep.
You say you want the facts?
And Judas says all those things?
Well, stand here. I'm busy
And have nothing at all to feed you.

Hate Judas? Me?
Oh, I think not.
But I have always known he seeks
Merely Justice and Order and that's
The defect central to his character.

The worthy rejoice
In the dunnage of God's
Love, but Judas refutes complicity,
And compares his rents to those
Who hold more properties than his woman

So Judas feels
Not paid enough—by God.
Embroiled thus, Love's other
Kingdoms elude each day the viper
Of his strong, unseemly intellect.

Judas alone
Would say The Master *used*
Women, for His ulterior motives.
Precludes compassion. The Master loved
The purity of women implied by their weeping,

But—I grant—
Your epigraph on "Little
Faith" is apt. I can feel
Precisely that in each cock-crow
Watch of my private, unaltered approbation.

Too little faith:
That's what we all had,
And by comparison had none at all
Until the delirium of palm fronds
By Gethsemane clawed and then convulsed us.

Oh, I'll confess
I will seldom go now
Inside any garden. Yet, daily,
I bear witness that our "Little
Faith" confounds the tackle of our intellect

Until it seems
This room and all these vast
Tactile ministries of the sun
Shall one day be consumed by Faith
Rampant, at last, above all rancored wilderness . . .

His great appeal?
Why, I should say The Master
Exploited practicality, exhumed
From mere rhetoric the felicities
Denied to parchment, and certain Pharisees.

Which is to say
The Master knew all rampant
Caste, horded wisdom, and by absence
Of parable monopolized all God's love,
Denied prodigality of loaves to multitudes.

Instead, The Master
Said He, alone, was God's
Son. And by example proved
His own allegations by bringing the tongues
Of His Father's own cross-weighted love to earth.

Say more? Me?
By way of qualification?
Well, put down that certain Scribes
Are also upright. Say Judas is admirable
In all the little ways we always knew . . .

Still the malicious
Becomes the omniscient and Judas
Yet may fall with his fine wool robes flapping
Into some undreamed garden of surrender . . .
Meanwhile, night is here. Goodbye. Work to do.

ENVOI

H
e
r
e

E
n
d

The Poems
of
JAMES B. HALL

Young at Hunt
Old at War
Drank Enough
And This Is All